William Shakespeare

by GEOFFREY EARLE
illustrated by ROGER HALL

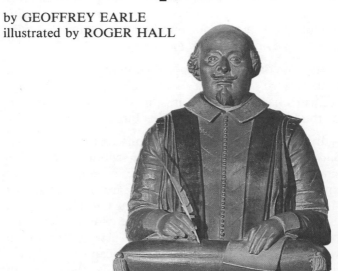

gh

Shakespeare's Life

In April 1564 a son was born to John and Mary Shakespeare at Henley Street, Stratford-on-Avon. His mother was the daughter of Robert Arden of Wilmcote, a considerable landowner in the county of Warwickshire; his father a prosperous citizen.

Neither could possibly have guessed, as they looked at the infant lying there in a wooden cradle on rockers, that he was to make such a tremendous gift to English poetry and drama, and that the plays he was to write would still be acted four hundred years later, not only in England, but all over the world.

In those days many babies died in infancy (as indeed Shakespeare's two elder sisters did) but young William seems to have flourished in spite of a severe outbreak of the Plague in the year of his birth.

In the play *As You Like It,* one of the characters, Jaques, talks about 'the whining schoolboy, with his satchel, and shining morning face, creeping like snail unwillingly to school'. Shakespeare was probably thinking of himself on his way to the Grammar School at Stratford when he wrote those words. True, no record of his attendance there survives, and you wouldn't find the initials W.S. carved on the lid of a desk, but it is as certain as can be that as the son of an important Stratford citizen he would have gone there and received a sound grounding in the classics. His friend Ben Jonson, another famous playwright, who admired him tremendously, says, however, he had 'small Latin and less Greek'.

There was some excuse for the schoolboy's unwillingness. He had a long, hard day starting at 6am in the summer and 7am in the winter; most people rose early in those days. Two or three hours' work was done before breakfast at 9, and there was a break for dinner at 11. Then back to school again at 1pm for another four hours till 5pm — by which time any boy would have been glad to get home!

When William was a schoolboy he would have had plenty of chance of seeing plays and meeting some of the touring companies of actors who went round the country, perhaps escaping from London when the Plague was rife. There were some local theatricals too, just as there are now in many towns. Stratford had its annual pageant of St George and the Dragon as well as the old mummers' play of St George, performed at Christmas (*shown above*).

All this may have sown the seeds of a love of the theatre which was to blossom so richly later when William went to London.

Meanwhile, he stayed at home and, while still a 'teenager' of 19, married Anne Hathaway, a farmer's daughter some years older than himself. Of course he had no house of his own, and probably took his bride to his father's house in Henley Street. It was then quite usual for two families to live together.

We don't know how he earned his living during these early years. He may have helped his father in the family business of glover, wool merchant and butcher, or he may have been a country schoolmaster for a time. Possibly he worked in a lawyer's office, where he could have picked up the many legal terms to be found in his plays. During these years three children were born: Susanna the eldest, then twins — a son Hamnet and another girl, Judith.

William was quite a lively young man and seems to have got mixed up with some other 'likely lads' in poaching escapades. The deer in Sir Thomas Lucy's park at Charlecote nearby were very tempting! Sir

Thomas was angry and threatened to prosecute him. He was even more angry when he found a rude verse fixed to his park gates:

'A parliament member, a justice of peace
At home a poor scarecrow, in London an asse
If Lucy is Lowsie as some folk miscall it
Sing Lowsie Lucy whatever befall it.'

Altogether, William had made Stratford too hot to hold him. He went off to London, leaving Anne and the children at home.

This was in 1587, a year when several companies of actors visited Stratford. William may have gone with one of them, or soon got in touch with some of the actors with whom he had made friends.

9

Shakespeare had been used to the rural life of Stratford, and must have found London very strange at first, for it was the biggest town in Europe. During his time there, its population increased to three hundred thousand people. (It's now over seven million.)

It was a walled city with gates, the names of some of which still survive in the names of London districts: Aldgate, Ludgate, Bishopsgate. It was also a town full of noise and bustle, with people thronging the narrow streets, and street vendors calling their wares. The bells of a hundred city churches could be heard, with St Paul's, at the top of Ludgate Hill, dominating all. Not, of course, the great domed cathedral built by Sir Christopher Wren that we know, but the old St Paul's that Shakespeare knew, which was destroyed by the Great Fire of 1666. St Paul's churchyard and the central aisle of the cathedral itself (Paul's Walk, it was called) was a great meeting place where men of fashion, wits, and City merchants gathered for business and gossip.

London was a great city of business. The merchants carried on their trade with many countries of Europe, whose ships could come up the Thames almost to the city. The Thames was a busy river, with watermen plying for hire up and down, or ferrying their passengers across to the south bank for the playhouse. The streets were so choked with filth and garbage that people often preferred to go by water.

There was only one bridge across the river – London Bridge, with twenty one piers and twenty arches. Boats could go under it, but only at the risk of meeting disaster in the turbulent waters and swirling current beyond. The bridge was almost like another street, with arched entrances and tall houses and shops from end to end on both sides.

The citizens of London lived in houses several storeys high, built of timber frames filled with clay and laths. The upper storeys jutted out so much that they made the narrow streets dark, and the half-timbered houses were closely packed together with little idea of planning. It was not surprising that when the Plague broke out (as it did almost every year) it spread very quickly. Smallpox was a common disease also.

There was no sanitation. Water had to be either brought by water carrier from a conduit fed from the river, or fetched from a well which might contain all sorts of impurities. Lighting was mainly by candles, and at night the narrow streets were dark except for the occasional faint glimmer of a horn lamp hanging outside a house. Rich people had carpets, but most people had rushes strewn on the floor as the only covering.

People of the nobility and upper classes at this time dressed rather extravagantly. The men wore doublet and hose. The doublet, of velvet, taffeta or silk, was a close-fitting waisted jacket worn over a shirt. It was padded and slashed with coloured ribbons for ornament. The breeches were usually very wide and padded. A short cloak of rich and colourful fabric, often hanging from only one shoulder, completed this picture of a fashionable *gallant,* a rich young man, perhaps on his way to a play at Shakespeare's theatre.

Both men and women wore ruffs. The ruff was a wide collar of linen or lace in the form of a frill, worn close to the neck. Women wore their ruffs cut lower in front and rising high at the back, almost like a frame for the head. Queen Elizabeth's ruffs were famous. Women's dress was just as gorgeous as the men's. Their clothes were made of velvet, damask or silk, richly ornamented with jewels. The narrow-waisted full skirts were worn over a farthingale (a padded hoop worn round the hips).

Shoes were very elegant. They had blunt toes, no heels, and a great deal of decoration on the fronts, which were high-cut (almost up to the ankle) and often had a ribbon tied round, ending in a butterfly bow. Even poor people liked to wear decorated shoes.

Merchants dressed more soberly, with hip or knee length tunics and a long sleeveless cloak. All their clothes were made from much simpler materials: wool or coarse linen cloth. Working people wore short smocks or belted tunics down to the knee, of canvas, leather or wool in drab colours.

Farthingale

15

Shakespeare, at the theatre or when the players visited the Court, must have come across all these different types of costume, but from portraits of him it seems that he dressed fairly quietly. He was too busy with his poetry and his plays to bother much about fashion.

There were only three theatres in London when he arrived there: The Theatre and The Curtain in the northern suburbs, and The Rose on the south bank of the River Thames near the Bear Garden. A brutal but very popular spectacle took place at the Bear Garden. Ferocious English mastiffs, kept specially for the purpose, were set on bears, which were usually chained up so that they couldn't escape. Often the dogs were killed, but they certainly showed courage in keeping up the attack on the bears. Shakespeare didn't seem to mind the hullabaloo there must have been, with the roaring and barking and the excited shouting of the rowdy

audience, for he had lodgings nearby. He must have seen this barbarous 'sport', and he refers to it in two of his plays – *Macbeth* and *Henry V*. Macbeth says, 'They have tied me to a stake; I cannot fly, but bear-like I must fight the course,' and in *Henry V* the mastiffs are described as 'Foolish curs! that run winking into the mouth of a Russian bear and have their heads crushed like rotten apples'.

Actors were classed as 'rogues and vagabonds' unless they were members of some nobleman's company and enjoyed his patronage and protection. Elizabeth herself had her own company of the Queen's Players. The Puritans thought actors wicked and sinful and did all they could to harass them and stop them performing. The rich City merchants despised them, too, and objected to the rowdiness that the crowds who came to the theatre sometimes caused. So the theatres grew up on the South Bank, away from the City, and were very popular with Elizabethan audiences.

Two stories are told about Shakespeare's early life in the theatre. It is said that he started by looking after the horses of people who came to the play on horseback (there were not many coaches then); and that later he was employed inside, possibly as a sort of 'callboy', whose job it was to tell the actors when to get ready to go on the stage and play their part.

Perhaps these stories are not true, but we know for certain that he soon began both to act and to write and adapt plays. By 1592 he was well established as a member of the Lord Chamberlain's Company. It was at this time that he made friends with two well known actors, Edward Alleyn, who founded Dulwich College, and Richard Burbage. In 1599, Richard and his brother Cuthbert built The Globe Theatre on the South Bank not far from the notorious Bear Garden. Shakespeare took a share in the venture with another well known actor, William Kemp, and others. It was in this theatre that most of his plays were performed.

Shakespeare as 'callboy'

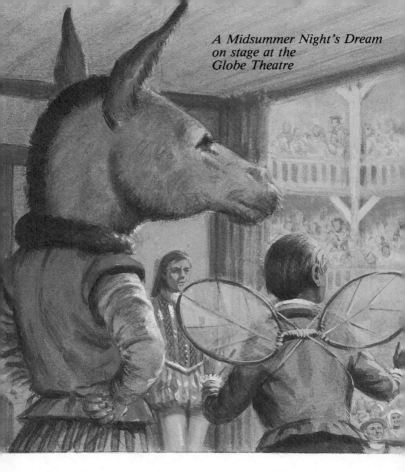

The Elizabethan theatre was quite unlike the theatre we know today. It was built of wood, round or octagonal in shape and open to the sky. The stage on which most of the action took place jutted out into the audience who stood all round. They were known as the groundlings, and paid only one penny. There were

covered galleries for those who could afford another penny or two, so these 'gallery commoners' had some protection from the weather. Some young gallants sat on stools actually on the stage. If they didn't like the play they stumped out of the theatre: very disconcerting for the actors!

At the back of the stage was a curtained recess. When the curtains were drawn apart this could be used whenever the scene was set in an inner room, such as Juliet's tomb, Desdemona's bed-chamber or Prospero's cell.

Above that was an upper storey which served as the balcony to which Romeo climbed to see his Juliet. It might represent the battlements of the castle where Richard II would appear when surrendering to Henry Bolingbroke standing in the courtyard below. Again perhaps it could be used for the window of Jessica's room in Shylock's house: from it she climbed down to run away with her lover, Lorenzo.

Romeo and Juliet

There was little or no scenery, though the actors' costumes were rich and magnificent. So the audience had to make much more use of their imaginations. Shakespeare helped them wherever he could. In *Henry V,* each Act is introduced by a character Shakespeare calls the 'Chorus' (we should call him a 'Narrator' today). He starts by apologising to the audience and asks:

'. . . can this cockpit hold
The vasty fields of France? or may we cram
Within this wooden O the very casques
That did affright the air at Agincourt?'

Often Shakespeare gives the audience a clue as to the place or time of day it is supposed to be. In *As You Like It,* for example, the heroine, Rosalind, leaves home with her friend, Celia, and goes to the forest where Celia's banished father is living.

As they enter (onto a bare stage, don't forget) Rosalind says, 'Well, this is the forest of Arden,' to which comes the reply, 'Ay, now am I in Arden.'

The wooded country north of Stratford was called Arden, and when Shakespeare set the scene of this play in the forest of Arden he was, no doubt, remembering his own native woodland.

In many plays he helps the audience to realise what time of day it is. In *Julius Caesar,* the conspirators, plotting to kill Caesar, meet in Brutus's orchard just before day-break. They argue amongst themselves as to exactly where the east is, and where the sun will rise.

'Here lies the east: doth not the day break here?
. . . and yon grey lines
That fret the clouds are messengers of day.'

That leaves no doubt that it is just before sunrise.

How could the dramatist create, on a bare stage in broad daylight, the illusion of a shattering storm? Listen to King Lear:

'Blow, winds, and crack your cheeks! rage! blow!
You cataracts and hurricanoes, spout
Till you have drench'd our steeples . . .,
Rumble thy bellyful! Spit, fire! Spout, rain!'

25

It was a rough, tough, even barbarous age, when people enjoyed brutal 'sports' like bear and bull baiting. Hanging was the penalty just for petty theft and for highway hold-ups on the rough and muddy roads that led to London. Public executions were a popular spectacle; traitors were dragged off to the Tower and beheaded, their heads exhibited stuck on pikes at the entrance to London Bridge. People were used to violence, bloodshed and death, and this was reflected in the plays of the age, particularly in Shakespeare's great tragedies.

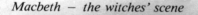

Macbeth — the witches' scene

There was *Hamlet*, with its theme of revenge and its ghost, murders and madness; *Macbeth* with murders again, the ghost of Banquo and the three weird and evil witches; in *Othello* Desdemona is violently killed by her husband; *King Lear* tells a story of madness and death; in *Romeo and Juliet* the young lovers die a tragic death; Cleopatra commits suicide.

27

All this sounds like mere 'blood and thunder' melodrama, but though the audience got the violence and bloodshed they wanted and seemed to like, they also got, by way of contrast, the wonderful poetry and music so characteristic of the Elizabethan period.

The Queen herself encouraged music and drama at her Court. Every young man was expected to take his part in singing a madrigal at sight, and perform on the lute. At least one of Shakespeare's plays was given its first performance before the Queen. Later, he enjoyed royal patronage when King James took over his company of actors and they became the King's men.

In all the comedies there are songs expressing the atmosphere of the play; love songs and songs of the woodland and country. Here again, Shakespeare drew on his own memories of spring and summer in the Warwickshire countryside of Arden.

Shakespeare had arrived in London at an exciting time, when the golden age of Elizabeth was at its peak.

It was just before the Great Armada set sail from Spain. The English seamen were adventuring everywhere – Hawkins, Raleigh, Drake. Drake had 'singed the King of Spain's beard' when he raided Cadiz, and with his fire-ships destroyed many ships and stores being prepared for the Armada. The Great Armada itself was destroyed in 1588. England seemed on the crest of a wave of success and achievement. No wonder there was a feeling of intense pride and patriotism among the robust and vigorous people.

Some great men of Shakespeare's time

Ben Jonson (1573-1637), actor and playwright
When he produced his comedy Every Man in his Humour *at the Curtain Theátre in 1598, Shakespeare was one of the actors*

Sir Francis Drake (1540-1596) was the first Englishman to sail round the world. His daring and courage were notable even in an age of brave men

Sir Walter Raleigh (1552-1618). He was the darling of Queen Elizabeth until he secretly married one of her maids of honour, when the Queen imprisoned them both in the Tower of London

Philip II of Spain He was married to Queen Elizabeth's sister, Mary Tudor. When she died in 1558, he tried unsuccessfully to marry Elizabeth. He later tried to conquer England, but his Great Armada of ships was defeated by Sir Francis Drake

31

Shakespeare sensed the feeling of pride and began to satisfy it by starting on the first of his series of historical plays, which eventually covered the whole background to the splendid Elizabethan age, from King John to Henry VIII, Elizabeth's father.

The source he used for these plays was Holinshed's *Chronicles*. This early history, published in 1587, gave him the facts he needed but with his great poetic gifts he transformed the dull prose of the *Chronicles* into the wonderful poetry which runs through all his plays like a rich vein of gold.

Henry VIII,
Queen Elizabeth's father

As You Like It

As well as the great poetic dramas of the historical plays and the tragedies such as *Hamlet* and *Macbeth* which he created, Shakespeare wrote a third type of play: romantic comedies such as *As You Like It* and *Twelfth Night*.

Since there were no actresses at that time (women did not appear on the stage until after the restoration of Charles II in 1660), all the female parts were played by boys. Elizabethan audiences loved the fun of cases of mistaken identity, but it does sound complicated — a boy pretending to be a woman disguised as a man, as happens in several of the comedies.

By 1611, Shakespeare was at the height of his powers. In the twenty four years he had been in London he had produced a prodigious output of thirty six plays, two long narrative poems and one hundred and fifty sonnets, as well as other poems. In addition he had been acting and sharing in the management of the Globe Theatre, and later of the Blackfriars when the Globe was burned down.

This happened in 1613, ten years after King James had come to the throne and had taken Shakespeare's company under his patronage as the King's men.

During a performance of *Henry VIII*, the last of the historical plays, stage cannons were fired in salute on Henry's entrance. A wad from one of them set fire to the thatch, and within an hour the theatre was burned to the ground. Surprisingly, no one was hurt, but an account of the fire tells us that 'one man had his breeches set on fire that would perhaps have broiled him, if he had not (by the benefit of a provident wit) put it out with bottle ale!'

Artist's impression of New Place

In an age when few men reached sixty, Shakespeare at fifty probably thought it time to retire. He had prospered, as well he deserved to. His family had been granted a coat of arms in 1596, but his pleasure at this had been marred by the death of his only son, Hamnet, in that year.

In 1597 he bought New Place, the finest house in Stratford, and also other property in London. During all these years he had been backwards and forwards to Stratford when he could get away from his busy life in London. Now it was time to retire for good to New Place, after he had written his last great romantic comedy or drama – *The Tempest*, a play full of beautiful poetry and some lovely songs.

He kept in touch with his friends in London and they came to visit him when he was installed at New Place. After a 'merry meeting' with two friends, Michael Drayton and Ben Jonson, Shakespeare contracted a fever of which he died on Tuesday, 23rd April – St George's Day – 1616. Two days later he was borne to the church where, as a baby, he had been christened.

His grave bears this inscription:

> 'Good friend, for Jesu's sake forbear
> To dig the dust enclosed here!
> Blest be the man that spares these stones
> And curst be he that moves my bones.'

And no one ever has!

There is also a worthy monument to him in the church. In an arched niche with marble pillars there is a bust of the poet, sitting with paper at hand and quill pen poised as if to write some immortal poetry, and underneath are these words:

> 'Stay passenger, why goest thou by so fast?
> Read if thou canst whom envious death hath placed
> Within this monument, Shakespeare, with whom
> Quick nature dide: whose name doth deck this tomb
> Far more than cost: sith all that he has writ
> Leaves living art but page to serve his wit.'

Perhaps the best epitaph of all is that of his friend and fellow playwright, Ben Jonson: 'He was not of an age, but for all time!' Prophetic words!

39

Shakespeare's Stratford

Today, because Shakespeare's plays and poetry are known and loved throughout the world, people travel thousands of miles to visit his birthplace in Stratford on Avon to do homage to his memory. There they can see the streets that he walked, with many buildings just as he knew them, the gardens that he loved, and countryside and villages close by that have changed little since his lifetime.

The Stratford that Shakespeare knew was much smaller than it is today however, although it was even then one of Warwickshire's most important market towns. At that time, its population was less than two thousand people — today it is ten times that number.

The photograph (*left*) shows the house in Henley Street where Shakespeare was born. It now stands on its own, but in Shakespeare's time it was part of a continuous frontage of houses and shops. Although there have been changes over the years, the house still looks much as it did originally.

The bedroom shown left is over the living-room — this is where tradition has it that Shakespeare was born. It is furnished in the fashion of Shakespeare's time.

41

Although Holy Trinity Church (*shown left*) has many other claims to fame, it is here that Shakespeare was both baptised and buried.

Among the church's most priceless possessions is the Parish Register, which contains the records of Shakespeare and his family, and also the font in which Shakespeare was baptised.

The Guildhall, Grammar School and almshouses of Stratford are shown below. Although there is no record of Shakespeare having attended the Grammar School, there is a strong likelihood that he did so. A school desk dating from his time is to be seen in his Birthplace.

The Grammar School itself (or its predecessor) was in existence by the end of the 13th century and was refounded by King Edward VI in 1553 (the year that Stratford became a borough).

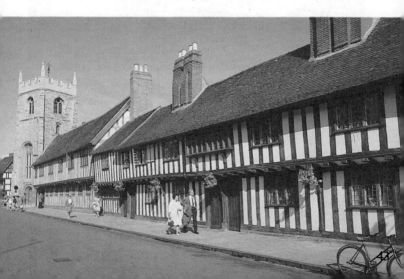

Anne Hathaway's Cottage

Anne Hathaway married Shakespeare in 1582, when she was 26. Up to that time she lived at Shottery, just over a mile to the west of Stratford on Avon. The oldest part of her cottage dates back to the fifteenth century, and most of the present furnishings actually belonged to the Hathaways and their descendants. The kitchen (*bottom picture*) still has its oven for bread-baking.

Mary Arden's House

Shakespeare's mother was Mary Arden, daughter of Robert Arden, and her home at Wilmcote has been preserved by the Shakespeare Birthplace Trust. It is a Tudor farmhouse built in the early 16th century, and there has been very little change in the house since Shakespeare's day. The living-room, shown here, is furnished in keeping.

The large entrance hall shown here leads to Susanna's kitchen and the staircase. The fireplace is a noteworthy feature.

Hall's Croft

This view of Hall's Croft, one of the finest Tudor houses to survive in Stratford, shows the long herbaceous border which leads from the terrace at the back of the house. The spacious garden is the only Shakespearian garden enclosed by a wall all round.

Shakespeare's elder (and favourite) daughter Susanna, and her husband Dr John Hall, lived here until Shakespeare's death in 1616, when they moved to New Place.

Here is the dispensary: the drug jars, herbs and medical equipment are very much as Dr Hall might have left them.

The Great Garden, New Place

The original kitchen garden and orchard belonging to New Place now form the Great Garden, shown above.

Here there is a mulberry tree grown from a cutting of a tree planted by Shakespeare himself. His original mulberry tree flourished for over a hundred years, but was cut down in 1756 by order of the Rev Francis Gastrell, who owned New Place at that time. This was

because the number of visitors to see the tree had begun to annoy him.

Later, when he had New Place demolished, he was forced to leave Stratford because of the anger of the townsfolk.

Shakespeare must have been well acquainted with the fourteen arches of Clopton Bridge (*below*), for the bridge was built at the end of the fifteenth century, about seventy years before he was born in 1564. It was given to Stratford by Hugh Clopton, a native of the town, who became Lord Mayor of London.

A Living Memorial

Few great men have been honoured with a living memorial such as the Royal Shakespeare Theatre in Stratford on Avon, shown above. Many of the most famous actors and actresses of today can claim the privilege of having appeared on its boards, and no visit to Stratford is complete without enjoying a performance there.

The theatre is one of the most modern and well equipped in the world, seating fifteen hundred people. The annual Shakespeare season lasts for ten months, during which a selection of probably five of

INDEX

Shakespeare's plays are performed 'in repertory'. This allows visitors to Stratford the opportunity to see more than one play during a short stay.

In today's productions, the use of sophisticated lighting techniques, imaginative costumes and skilful stage designs, all help to create the right mood and atmosphere.

Shown below is a scene from one of the Royal Shakespeare Theatre's productions of *The Merry Wives of Windsor*